AF578888

LEARN TO READ

(An Intervention Reading Material for Elementary

MARIZA JOY B. ABALOS
Master Teacher I
Camiing Elementary School

COPYRIGHT 2023 LEARN TO READ
By MARIZA JOY B. ABALOS

All rights reserved. No part of this publication may be produced, distributed, or transmitted in any form or any means, including photocopying, recording, or other electronic or mechanical methods without the prior permission of the publisher and author, except in the case of brief quotations embodied in critical reviews and certain other commercial uses permitted by copyright law may be reproduced or used in any manner without the prior written permission of the copyright owner and publisher.

ISBN
Hardbound-978-621-470-854-3
Softbound/Paperback-978-621-470-855-0
MOBI/KINDLE-978-621-470-856-7

Published by:
Poetry Planet Book Publishing House
Rosario, Pozorrubio, Pangasinan, Philippines
Contact Number: 09554960094
Email: maritesritumalta@gmail.com

a
an
and
away
big
blue
can
one
come
up
for
all
am
are
at
ate

down
I
go
help
in
two
to
into
is
here
help
be
black
get
four
he

jump
long
me
not
run
you
see
the
we
three
red
no
now
on
our
have

too
ran
so
she
say
soon
that
there
they
how
my
it
eat
but
did
do

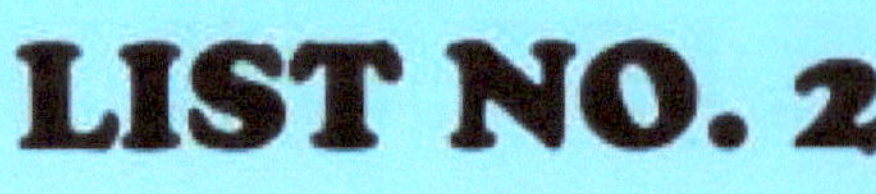

LIST NO. 2

- out
- get
- good
- like
- must
- new
- yellow
- where
- run
- please
- pretty
- ride
- saw
- this
- under
- want

- was
- well
- went
- what
- white
- brown
- air
- who
- will
- with
- yes
- after
- again
- any
- ask
- as

- by
- can
- every
- fly
- give
- from
- going
- had
- has
- her
- him
- his
- how
- just
- let
- live

- may
- of
- old
- once
- over
- open
- put
- stop
- some
- take
- thank
- them
- then
- think
- walk
- were

when	been	sit	about
round-	because	sleep	better
fast	around	tell	bring
first	always	fell	carry
five	found	their	clean
give	goes	these	cut
off	green	those	done
gave	its	upon	draw
does	made	use	drink
don't	many	very	eight
cold	make	wash	could
call	pull	which	would
buy	read	wish	fall
both	right	work	full
best	sing	why	far
before	dance	your	get

- got
- grow
- hold
- hot
- hurt
- if
- bad
- keep
- kind
- write
- light
- pretty
- much
- myself
- never
- only

- own
- pick
- seven
- shall
- show
- six
- small
- start
- ten
- today
- try
- warm
- across
- address
- ago
- airplane

- also
- aunt
- ant
- awake
- bake
- banana
- bath
- beans
- beat
- began
- bend
- beside
- between
- bill
- bit
- blow

- center
- case
- cause
- care
- careful
- cap
- camp
- button
- busy
- built
- building
- bone
- born
- bow
- bottom
- brave

- break
- brick
- broke
- broken
- brought
- bug
- building
- beautiful
- chimney
- city
- chin-
- cloud
- clock
- cook
- cool
- count

- country
- creek
- cover
- course
- cough
- cross
- cup
- dear
- dead
- desk
- deer
- different
- dice
- dirty
- dream
- drop

- dark
- deaf
- dry
- dust
- drum
- dried
- dig
- east
- early
- else
- edge
- enough
- even
- eye
- enter
- exit

- epic
- entire
- eldest
- exile
- elf
- eager
- family
- feather
- fantasy
- feel
- felt
- few
- fight
- field
- finger
- foot

fresh
fur
front
fry
filter
fund
flower
friend
free
freedom
fried
fog
father
gift
god
gone

gray
grew
grass
great
grid
grand
giraffe
giant
gear
grind
graph
hair
hall
half
heavy
hang

herself
hid
himself
hundred
hole
hung
hungry
hate
hunter
hug
hard
keep
kept
kick
kitten
kiss

knew
knife
knock
kite
kettle
land
lake
lap
large
lead
late
leaf
leaves
leave
learn
led

LIST NO. 7

lift	miss	number	pie
left	most	narrow	piece
line	mouth	navigate	place
listen	Mr.	outside	plain
loud	Mrs.	oven	plant
lost	margin	open	plate
lion	merit	orbit	pond
letter	marry	page	poor
matter	mighty	pail	pot
march	mint	path	press
mark	neck	pen	pride
mean	nap	peace	panel
minute	need	peas	parent
meat	nice	pay	queen
meet	nine	pencil	quick
middle	nothing	people	question

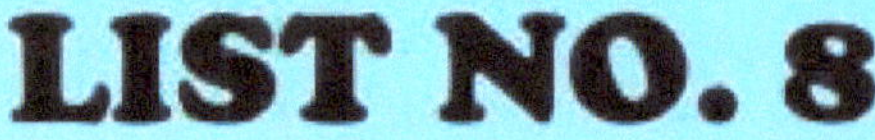

- quiet
- quit
- radio
- ready
- read
- real
- really
- rich
- river
- rock
- roof
- row
- raw
- rotten
- range
- ripe
- save
- sand
- seat
- seem
- seen
- send
- shake
- shine
- shook
- shape
- should
- scape
- skip
- shut
- side
- silver
- skin
- sky
- slope
- slip
- sleep
- slow
- smile
- smoke
- soap
- socks
- soft
- some
- sound
- space
- soup
- spot
- stairs
- stand
- station
- stay
- still
- sting
- stand
- stood
- story
- straight
- strong
- such
- suit
- super
- supper
- suppose

sure
sweep
sweet
touch
teach
teeth
than
thin
thought
through
throw
till
tired
trade
tried
true

twelve
twin
twilight
thread
trumpet
treasure
teacher
tomato
thorn
toes
treat
table
wake
wall
wave
whisper

wear
week
winter
west
while
win
wing
without
wonder
warmth
watch
waive
waffle
waddle
warden
weaken

wool
world
want
wash
wander
wind
wig
yet
yacht
year
yoga
yolk
youth
yeast
yule
yawn

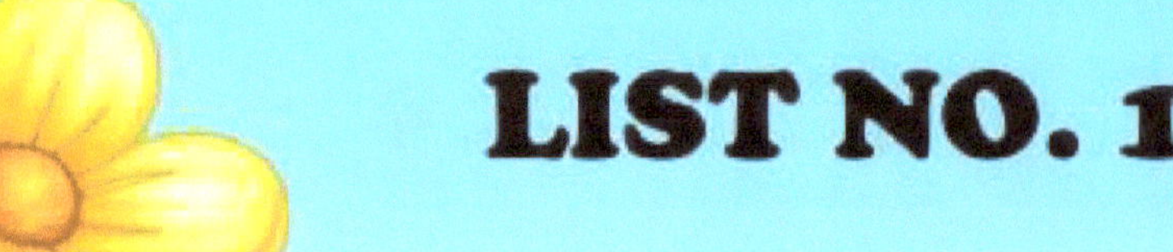

ache
act
after
against
alone
already
answer
arm
ban
bank
bathe
begin
began
believe
board
bleed

blind
blood
body
bow
bridge
broom
bump
burnt
butcher
butter
captain
careless
catch
chain
chalk
chance

change
cheek
chief
child
choose
church
circle
class
clear
cloth
cocoa
copy
cost
cough
cousin
crackers

crayons
crowd
crown
cry
curtain
danger
date
dentist
die
dining
dinner
dirt
doctor
double
drawer
drug

LIST NO. 11

eraser	furniture	iron	leather
either	garage	image	lemon
end	gate	insect	lesson
evening	glad	ivory	lettuce
except	golden	index	lie
expect	grade	input	lip
fair	grain	ideal	load
feeding	grocery	idiom	low
fellow	guess	juice	mailman
fill	hammer	jewel	market
finish	heard	jeans	measure
follow	heart	knee	mend
following	hour	knock	mile
fork	ice	lady	mind
forth	indoor	lamp	month
fourth	instead	laid	mount

LIST NO. 12

move	overall	rather	scooter
music	pain	reach	season
napkin	pants	reason	self
nickel	pass	rest	sent
neither	past	ribbon	serve
none	paste	road	several
noon	peach	room	shadow
nor	pillow	rooster	shape
north	point	root	ship
note	porch	rose	shirt
nurse	post	rubber	short
ocean	potato	rug	shoulder
office	pound	ruler	silk
often	puzzle	sail	sir
other	quarter	salt	size
ought	quiet	scissors	skirt

LIST NO. 13

sold	sweater	twenty	women
soldier	talk	ugly	worry
sore	taste	umbrella	wrap
south	tear	until	wrong
speak	thank	valley	zipper
spoke	thick	visit	admire
spoon	thirsty	wait	love
spread	throat	war	move
spring	thumb	waist	though
square	tire	waste	ought
start	tongue	weather	dough
stocking	touch	wheat	fright
stomach	tough	whether	light
stove	towel	whole	sigh
sugar	train	whom	system
summer	tub	whose	cyclone

LIST NO. 14

although	improbable	irregular
handkerchief	immature	irresponsible
campaign	imprison	irrational
chocolate	impractical	irreversible
hydrogen	impatient	irresistible
admirable	immoral	illogical
responsible	imprint	illegible
hydrant	improper	centigrade
foreign	buoy	encounter
coarse	impersonal	encourage
patience	immortal	enclose
receive	advertise	proceed
believe	addressed	committee
design	adapt	tomorrow
cruise	adjust	access
impossible	advance	accident

LIST NO. 15

progress
project
interrupt
intermission
interpret
international
circulate
circumference
international
circumstance
circus
incision
include
inhale
transcend
transfer

calculate
compute
diagram
telephone
divisible
thousand
equation
equivalent
evaluate
estimation
formula
kilometer
median
mean
polygon
probability

quotient
agriculture
industry
economics
bacteria
vineyard
government
history
astronomy
civilization
conservative
environment
government
minority
independent
hypothesis

Let's Read More

It's Fun

It's fun to run!

One, one one! It's fun to hop!
Please , don't stop!

It's fun to ride back home by bus.
It's fun to come to English class!

A Monster

A monster lives under my bed.
It doesn't like milk, doesn't like bread.
It doesn't like noise, doesn't like light.
It comes out only at night. It sits by the window looking so sad.

Let's Read More

Have a Look!

Have a look! Have a look!

It's a book. My new book! It's interesting. It's so nice! It's difficult but I have read it twice.

A Knight at Night

Once at night, a knight went out for a night. The night was dark. There was no light. Since then, no one has seen that knight.

www.ingramcontent.com/pod-product-compliance
Lightning Source LLC
LaVergne TN
LVHW071225160826
845679LV00003B/907
* 9 7 8 6 2 1 4 7 0 8 5 5 0 *